The Best in the World

FAST, HEALTHFUL RECIPES FROM EXCLUSIVE AND OUT-OF-THE-WAY RESTAURANTS

Edited by Neal D. Barnard, M.D.

PCRM
Washington, DC

Foreword

From a seaside cafe in Portugal, a cozy restaurant in Saint-Tropez, or a trendy night spot in Sydney, come recipes that truly are the best in the world.

Who would have expected to find the world's best gazpacho just off the Tuileries in Paris, the best burrito in Fargo, North Dakota, or the best minestrone in Munich? But here they are.

To be included in this collection, a recipe had to be delightful and reasonably quick to prepare. It also had to be healthful. After all, a dinner that reminds you to check your cholesterol can never be an unalloyed pleasure.

Many chefs work by "feel," taste, and intuition, without strict measurements. In testing these recipes, we have provided specific quantities and instructions, and a few have been adjusted to contain a chef's exuberance for olive oil, to use a binder other than eggs, or to make other modifications for health and convenience.

We owe a special thank you to the chefs and restaurateurs who kindly provided these wonderful creations. Thanks also to Elsie Quinn, Muriel DuCloy, Harald Ullman, and Liza Bigonzoli.

Miyun Park and Doug Hall provided the layout and design. Cathy DeLuca managed our team of talented recipe testers: Patricia Bertron, R.D., Ketti Goudey, Aaron Gross, Bonnie Kumer, R.D., Kate Schumann, and Robin Walker. Thanks to Vicki Baron for her lovely illustrations.

Neal D. Barnard, M.D.

Contents

CHATEAU DE LA MESSARDIERE

Appetizers

CHILLED MELON AND GRAPEFRUIT IN A MINT AND GINGER SAUCE

Chateau de la Messardiere, Saint-Tropez, France

SERVES 4

*C*hef Jean-Louis Vosgien conducts the Provence Cooking School at la Messardiere, a 19th century chateau now converted to a modern luxury hotel. To his natural genius and training, he adds the fruits of his annual trips to Asia, such as Thai sauces adapted to Provencal cuisine.

This light appetizer uses palm sugar, also called jaggery, which is made from palm trees and has a unique wine-like flavor. It is found in Indian markets, or you can use brown or even white sugar in its place.

FRUIT

2 pounds cantaloupe (or other muskmelon)
4 medium grapefruit, peeled, segmented, seeded, reserving juice

10 fresh mint leaves, crumbled
4 small mint bouquets (optional)

Scoop out cataloupe using a melon baller, or cut into 1/2-inch cubes. Divide the cantaloupe and grapefuit between four individual serving plates. Chill until ready to serve.

Just before serving, top with Mint and Ginger Sauce and sprinkle with mint. Garnish with mint bouquets.

MINT AND GINGER SAUCE

1 1/4 cups grapefruit juice
1 cup palm sugar or brown sugar

3/4 cup fresh lemon juice
2 tablespoons minced ginger

In a medium saucepan, add grapefruit juice, sugar, and lemon juice. Stir ingredients over medium heat until sugar is dissolved. Do not boil. Add ginger and chill 1–2 hours.

COURGETTES FARCIES

Cafe de Paris, Monte-Carlo, Monaco

SERVES 4

The Cafe de Paris spills out from the casino onto an airy veranda where sparrows and pigeons patiently wait for crumbs.

2 small or medium zucchini	1/3 cup chopped ripe black
1 tablespoon olive oil	olives

Wash zucchini and trim off ends. With a fork, score the zucchini lengthwise for decoration. Cut the zucchini into 1-inch cylinders and scoop out a hollow in one of the flat ends with a melon baller or grapefruit spoon. Place zucchini pieces in a steamer, hollowed side up, and steam for 4-5 minutes until crisp-tender, taking care not to let them get soggy. Remove from steamer and place upside down on a paper towel to remove excess liquid.

Mix olive oil and chopped olives. Stuff zucchini with a teaspoon of the olive mixture. Serve cold or at room temperature as an appetizer or along with cruditees as a salad course.

TERRINE DE POIRREAUX (LEEKS)

Restaurant Lou Marques, Arles, France

SERVES 4

The town of Arles, France, has a special air and light that greeted Vincent Van Gogh one snow-covered day in February, 1888. There, Van Gogh completed 190 paintings, including some of his best loved masterpieces.

This simple, delicate appetizer is made from cooked leeks which are pressed between two terrines. You can also use flat pans (one 9 x 12 inches, the other smaller), which can be set one inside the other.

4 medium leeks

Boil leeks 30 minutes in salted water, until soft. When done, they should give no resistance to a knife. Drain the leeks while still hot.

Place them in one terrine lengthwise, with the green end of the first leek on the left, the green end of the second on the right, and so on, creating an alternating color pattern. Then press the second terrine onto the leeks, and add a weight (about 20 pounds) on top. Leave overnight. Then cut into rectangles. Serve at room temperature with a vinaigrette sauce, on a bed of lettuce if you like. After dinner, enjoy a short drive down to the sea-shore.

STUFFED ARTICHOKE

Artichoke's Cafe, Palm Beach Gardens, Florida

This Thai/Japanese restaurant is perhaps the only place in the world where you can order a carrot juice or a kamikaze with equal ease.

4 artichokes
1 1/2 teaspoons soy margarine
1/2 teaspoon olive oil
2-3 cloves garlic, crushed
1/2 cup diced red peppers
1/2 cup sweet green peas
1/2 teaspoon dried basil
1/2 teaspoon dried oregano
12 ounces fresh spinach, coarsely chopped
1 tablespoon seasoned bread crumbs

Remove stems from artichokes. Place a steamer basket in a saucepan over boiling water. Add artichokes, reduce heat, and cover; steam for 40 minutes. Artichokes should be soft, but not mushy. Remove artichokes from the steamer and run under cold water to prevent the leaves from curling. Spread the leaves apart, and remove choke with a spoon. Set aside.

Heat soy margarine and olive oil in a large, non-stick skillet. Add garlic, red peppers, peas, basil, and oregano, and sauté over medium heat for 3 minutes. Add spinach and cover, stirring occasionally, for 3-4 minutes. Remove from heat and mix bread crumbs with spinach mixture. Divide into four portions and stuff into center of each artichoke. Serve with a sweetened mustard dip.

Artichokes can be prepared ahead of time and refrigerated. Reheat in microwave or low oven.

BRUSCHETTA

Piero's, Crown Casino, Melbourne, Australia

MAKES 1 1/2 CUPS

*A*t Melbourne's new Crown Casino, Piero's restaurant nurses gamblers' wounds with a traditional Italian starter that never tasted better.

1 cup diced tomatoes, hearts discarded
1/4 cup diced red onion
2 cloves garlic, minced
1/4 cup minced fresh parsley
1/4 cup minced fresh basil, minced
salt and pepper to taste

Combine tomatoes and next four ingredients in a square pan. Add salt and pepper to taste. Refrigerate until ready to serve. To serve, spoon onto thin slices of toasted baguette.

Bruschetta with Julienned Vegetables

MAKES 3 CUPS

1 cup julienned carrots
1 cup julienned zucchini
1 cup julienned squash
1/4 cup minced red onion
1/4 cup minced fresh parsley
1/4 cup minced fresh basil

1 tablespoon balsamic
 vinegar
1 tablespoon seasoned
 rice vinegar
1 tablespoon water
2 cloves garlic, minced

Combine carrots and next five ingredients in a small bowl. Whisk together balsamic vinegar, seasoned rice vinegar, water, and garlic. Pour vinegar mixture over vegetables and toss gently. Refrigerate until ready to serve. To serve, spoon onto thin slices of toasted baguette.

Soups and Chili

SOUPE DE LEGUMES

La Pesquiere, Saint-Tropez, France

SERVES 8

Saint-Tropez has lured sunbathers and yacht crews by the thousands since Brigitte Bardot made the quiet Cote d'Azur village her home in the 1950s. In the heart of the old village, Jacques Cadel runs two outstanding restaurants looking out over the Mediterranean. This soup of minced vegetables is delicate, but hearty.

1 tablespoon olive oil	2/3 cup diced onions
2 cups peeled and diced carrots	8 cups water
2 cups peeled and diced turnips	salt and pepper to taste
4 cups trimmed and diced leeks	

Heat olive oil in a large pot. Add carrots, turnips, leeks, potatoes, and onions, and sauté for 2 minutes over medium heat. Add 8 cups of water or enough to cover the vegetables. Add salt and pepper to taste. Bring to a boil, cover, reduce heat, and simmer for 1 1/2 hours or until vegetables are tender. Serve in individual bowls.

GAZPACHO

l'Absinthe, Paris, France

SERVES 4

*I*n a section of Paris featuring an odd mixture of Chinese, Japanese, and even Russian cuisine, the chef gives a French touch to a popular Spanish soup.

4 medium ripe tomatoes, diced
1 medium cucumber, peeled and
  diced
1 green pepper, seeded and diced
1 medium red onion, diced
1 clove garlic, crushed

salt and pepper to taste
juice of 1 lemon
1-2 cups tomato juice
pimentos to taste
Tabasco sauce to taste
crumbled cilantro to taste

In a large bowl, combine diced tomatoes and next seven ingredients and mix thoroughly. To serve, ladle into individual bowls and add pimentos and Tabasco sauce to taste. Garnish with cilantro.

TROPICAL FRUIT SOUP

Chadwick's, Captiva Island, Florida

SERVES 4

*D*uring the 1700s, pirate Jose Gaspar plundered the west coast of Florida. Legend has it that he kept his loot on Santa Isybella Island, now known as Sanibel, and his female captives on the nearby Isle de los Captivas, now called Captiva. Clarence, the original Chadwick, bought up the whole island and raised tropical fruits, the most famous of which were key limes.

1/2 canteloupe, peeled, seeded,
  and chopped
1/2 honeydew, peeled, seeded,

and chopped
1/2 cup orange juice
sugar (optional)

Place fruit in a blender or food processor. Add orange juice and pureé. Add sugar if necessary for not-quite-ripe fruit. Serve in individual bowls.

EL TERRAL

CREMA DE FRIJOLES NEGROS

El Terral, Las Hadas, Manzanillo, Mexico

SERVES 4-6

*L*as Hadas, on Mexico's Pacific coast, was made famous by Bo Derek and Dudley Moore the movie *10*. It is totally isolated from the surrounding Mexican countryside and culture, until you taste chef Alfredo Ponce's black bean soup—authentic and delicious. We have substituted soymilk for cream.

2 1/2 cups (1 pound) dried black beans	1 tablespoon olive oil
6-7 cups water	1 cup soymilk
3 cloves garlic, crushed	tortillas for garnish
1 1/2 teaspoon salt	lettuce for garnish

Soak beans overnight. Drain, and cover with water. Add the garlic and cook until soft, about 2 hours, or five minutes in a pressure cooker. Do not undercook. Blend the beans with the cooking water and return to pot. Reheat with salt, olive oil, and soymilk. Garnish with thinly sliced fried tortillas and strips of lettuce.

THE NEUTRAL BAY CLUB

Carrot Soup

The Neutral Bay Club, North Sydney, Australia

SERVES 12

This recipe comes from Geoff Bailey, at a bowling club not far from Sydney Harbor.

1 tablespoon olive oil
2 pounds (about 5 cups) peeled and sliced carrots
1 onion, chopped
2 medium potatoes, peeled and diced
6 cups water

2 cubes vegetable stock
1/2 teaspoon salt
1 teaspoon sugar
black pepper to taste
1 teaspoon mixed herbs
parsley to garnish

Heat oil in a large saucepan. Add vegetables and cook over medium heat, turning with a wooden spoon until thoroughly coated with oil. Add water, stock cubes, salt, sugar, pepper, and herbs. Simmer until tender. Put into a blender and whisk until smooth. Serve with parsley.

Special thanks to Ms. Elsie Quinn.

VEGETARIAN CHILI

Hard Times Cafe, Rockville, Maryland

SERVES 6

*C*incinnati chili keeps the Queen City warm and Texas chili may be why the state is a leader in heart disease research, but the Hard Times Cafe serves a terrific vegetarian chili, while Tammy Wynette croons from the juke box.

This recipe uses textured vegetable protein, made from defatted soy flour, which has a meaty texture when rehydrated in boiling water. It is an excellent meat substitute in sauces, chili, and stews, and is available in health food stores. The Hard Times offers pre-measured chili spice packets. Write to Hard Times Chili, 310 Commerce St., Alexandria, Virginia 22314. For a "veggie mac," serve chili over spaghetti noodles.

1 28-ounce can tomato sauce	1/3 cup chili powder
3 ounces tomato paste	1 1/2 teaspoons cumin
1/4 cup water	1 teaspoon crushed red pepper
1 cup texturized vegetable protein	2 teaspoons garlic powder
1 cup cooked and drained kidney beans	1 teaspoon oregano
4 ounces diced mushrooms	1/3 teaspoon allspice
1 green pepper, diced	salt to taste (optional)
1 jalapeno pepper, diced	chopped tomatoes (optional)
1 medium onion, finely chopped	chopped spinach (optional)

Place all ingredients in a large sauce pan. Bring to a boil, cover, reduce heat, and simmer for 2 to 2 1/2 hours or until lightly thickened. Refrigerate overnight. Reheat when ready to use. To serve, ladle into individual bowls, adding chopped tomatoes or spinach as desired.

LENTIL-SPINACH SOUP

Lulu's, Madison, Wisconsin

SERVES 8

*T*his recipe uses allspice as a garnish. If you prefer, you can use a mixture of white pepper, paprika, cinnamon, nutmeg, and cardamom.

1 tablespoon vegetable oil
salt to taste
1 large onion, chopped
5 cups water
1/3 cup basmati rice
2 cups dried brown lentils
2 cloves garlic, crushed

1 pound coarsely chopped fresh
    spinach
juice of 1 lemon
parsley, chopped (optional)
ground cumin (optional)
ground allspice (optional)

Heat oil and salt in a medium pot. Add onion and sauté over medium heat until tender. Add water and bring to a boil. Stir in rice and lentils and bring to a second boil. Cover, reduce heat, and simmer 45 minutes or until lentils and rice are soft, adding more water as needed. Add garlic, spinach, and lemon juice. Cover and cook for an additional five minutes until thoroughly heated. To serve, ladle into individual bowls and garnish chopped parsley, cumin and allspice.

SOPA DE LEGUMES

Restaurante Tamargueira, Figueira da Foz, Portugal

SERVES 4

*T*his hearty, simple soup is a staple of Portuguese cuisine.

1 large potato, chopped
2-3 carrots, chopped
1 large turnip, chopped
2-3 cups fresh chopped spinach or
other green vegetables

12-14 cups water
1 tablespoon olive oil
2 teaspoons salt
4 ounces spaghetti, broken
into 2-inch pieces

In a saucepan, boil potato, carrots, turnip, and green vegetables for 40 minutes. Then add olive oil and salt. Cool, then blend using a blender, food processor, or mixer. Add spaghetti. For a thicker soup, use less water. As a variation, add the green vegetables after thoroughly blending the other cooked ingredients, and only partially blend the green vegetables.

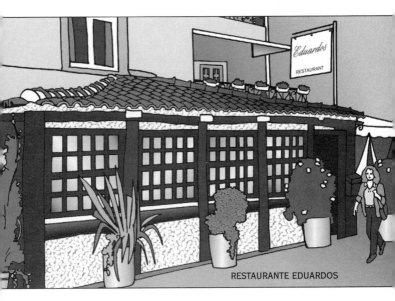

RESTAURANTE EDUARDOS

CALDO VERDE

Restaurante Eduardos, Cascais, Portugal

SERVES 4

This delicious, traditional soup recipe comes from Uwe Wenzel, a skilled chef from Germany, now delighting diners in Portugal. The name caldo verde refers to a deep green Portuguese cabbage which is sliced into long thin strips. If you happen not to live in Cascais and are having trouble finding this cabbage, you can substitute julienned white cabbage, kale, or collards, or even spinach in a pinch.

4 cups previously boiled potatoes
  (about 2 large potatoes)
1 onion, quartered
1 stalk celery, chopped
2 tablespoons olive oil
1 clove garlic, halved

4 cups julienned white
  cabbage, kale, or collards
1/4 teaspoon salt (optional)
1 teaspoon soy sauce (optional)
1 teaspoon maggi (optional)

Cover potatoes, onion, and celery with water. Add olive oil and garlic. Boil 30 minutes or more, then blend with a blender, food processor, or mixer. Then add white cabbage, kale, or collards. Cook 20 minutes more. Season with 1/4 teaspoon salt, 1 teaspoon soy sauce, or 1 teaspoon maggi, which is similar to soy sauce and found in Asian markets.

SOUPE CORSE

U Casanu, Calvi, Corsica

SERVES 6-8

*A*lthough a part of France, the island of Corsica is independent in many ways, not least of which is its cuisine. In Calvi, across from Place Marchal, where doves enjoy the fading light of a summer evening, the statue of Docteur Marchal, professor at the Faculty of Medicine of Paris in the mid-1800s, watches the restaurant, as if to appreciate the health benefits of the Soupe Corse.

1/2 cup dry kidney beans
8 cups vegetable broth
2 cups chopped Swiss chard
4 medium carrots, cut in 1/2-inch
  coins (2 cups)
2 medium leeks, chopped (2 cups)*
2 small zucchini, cut in 1/2-inch
coins (2 1/2 cups)
2 medium potatoes, cut into
  1" cubes (2 cups)
1/2 cup dry fusilli or other pasta
2 cloves garlic, finely chopped
1/4 cup fresh basil, chopped
salt to taste

Cover the kidney beans with water and soak overnight. Drain, rinse, and place in soup pot. Add vegetable broth, Swiss chard, carrots, leeks, zucchini, and potatoes. Bring to a boil, and cook for 1 hour. Add uncooked pasta, garlic, and basil. Simmer another 5-7 minutes to cook pasta to until almost tender. Add salt to taste.

* To wash leeks, trim off root ends and most of dark green. Split leeks lengthwise and hold under running water to remove any grit.

GREEN LENTIL SOUP

Le Commensal, Montreal, Quebec, Canada

SERVES 4

*P*our le plaisir de bien manger" are the words that have nourished Le Commensal into a group of popular restaurants in Quebec and Ontario. The Montreal restaurant spreads

LE COMMENSAL

a huge buffet of original dishes in a broad airy room that once housed a museum.

1 tablespoon sesame oil
1/3 cup diced red onions
1/2 cup green lentils
1 teaspoon thyme
1/2 teaspoon pepper
dash of cayenne
3 cups water
1/3 cup chopped celery

1/3 cup peeled and sliced
  carrots
1/3 cup peeled and diced
  turnips
1/3 cup diced cabbage
2 bay leaves
1 tablespoon tamari or to taste
1/2 teaspoon sea salt or to taste

Heat oil in a large saucepan. Add onions, lentils, thyme, pepper, and cayenne, and sauté for 2-3 minutes. Add water, celery, carrots, turnips, cabbage, and bay leaves. Bring to a boil, reduce heat, and simmer for 45 minutes or until the vegetables become tender. Add tamari and sea salt to taste. Serve hot.

APPLE AND PARSNIP SOUP

The Granville Hotel, Brighton, England

SERVES 4

*B*righton is a seaside town on England's south coast where work-weary Londoners can watch waves caress the pebbles on the shore. At the Granville Hotel, Sue Paskins serves up many vegan items, such as this Apple and Parsnip Soup.

1 tablespoon olive oil	2 medium cooking apples,
1 medium onion, chopped	chopped
2 medium parsnips, chopped	1/4 teaspoon nutmeg
4 cups vegetable stock	salt and pepper to taste

Heat oil in a medium-sized soup pot. Add the onion and parsnips and sauté for 5-7 minutes or until tender. Add the vegetable stock, apples, and nutmeg. Bring to a boil. Reduce heat, cover, and simmer for 30 minutes. In a food processor, pureé the soup. Taste and adjust seasonings as desired. Serve hot.

SOUPE DE LEGUMES AU PISTOU

La Feniera, Nice, France

SERVES 6-8

*A*ndre Mignon got this recipe from his mother, who served the dish as a country breakfast.

1/2 cup dry white beans	1/2 pound green beans, diced
8 cups unsalted vegetable broth	(1 1/2 cups)
2 tablespoons olive oil	1 medium tomato, diced (1 cup)
1 medium onion, diced (1 cup)	1/4 cup chopped fresh basil
3 medium garlic cloves, crushed	1/2 teaspoon salt
1 stalk celery, diced (1/2 cup)	fresh ground pepper to taste
1 medium potato, diced (1 cup)	1/2 cup dry fusilli or other
2 medium carrots, diced (1 cup)	fine pasta

Cover beans with water and soak overnight in refrigerator. Drain, rinse, and place in a soup pot. Add vegetable broth and bring to a boil, and simmer for 1 hour.

Meanwhile, heat oil in a large pan and sauté the onions gently for 5-7 minutes or until tender. Add garlic, followed by celery, potato, carrots, green beans, and tomato, and sauté for 5 more minutes and set aside.

When the beans have cooked for 1 hour, add the vegetables to the beans and continue simmering for another 20 minutes. Then add basil, salt, pepper, and pasta and cook for 5 more minutes or until the pasta is tender. Adjust salt and pepper to taste.

MINESTRONE

Restaurant Talamonti, Munich, Germany

SERVES 4

2 tablespoons and 6 cups vegetable broth	1 cup diced carrots
1 cup diced zucchini	1 medium potato, peeled and diced
2 cups diced green cabbage	1 teaspoon olive oil
2 cups chopped spinach	1 medium onion, chopped
2 cups sweet peas	salt and pepper to taste
2 cups chopped kale	balsamic vinegar to taste

Heat 2 tablespoons vegetable broth in a large non-stick skillet. Add vegetables and cook for 5 minutes. Remove from heat and set aside.

Heat 1 teaspoon olive oil in a large saucepan over high heat. Add onion and sauté for several minutes until brown. Add remaining vegetable broth and vegetable mixture. Add salt and pepper to taste. Bring to a boil, reduce heat, cover, and simmer for 15-20 minutes or until potatoes are cooked. Ladle into individual bowls. Add a dash of balsamic vinegar. Serve hot.

CORN AND POTATO CHOWDER

Artichoke's Cafe, Palm Beach Gardens, Florida

SERVES 6

1/2 yellow onion, chopped
1 cup chopped cabbage
1 teaspoon soybean or olive oil
1 bay leaf
1/4 teaspoon whole celery seed
1/4 teaspoon white pepper
2 teaspoons chopped fresh garlic
1 teaspoon tamari
1/2 carrot, shredded

3-4 baking potatoes, peeled and diced
1/2 cup corn
1/2 cup peas (optional)
1 cup soymilk
1/2 teaspoon salt, or to taste
1 tablespoon arrowroot or cornstarch

Sauté onion and cabbage in oil with bay leaf, celery seed, pepper, and garlic, until onions are translucent and well cooked. Add tamari. Then add shredded carrot, potatoes, and cold water to cover. Bring to a boil and cook until just tender. Add corn, and peas if desired. Add soy milk, and salt to taste. Thicken by dissolving a bit of arrowroot or cornstarch into a small amount of liquid, and adding back to the soup.

Salads

SALADE PRINTONIERE AUX POINTES D'ASPERGE

Le Cafe Drouant, Paris, France

SERVES 4

At the Cafe Drouant every spring, the prestigious literary Prix Goncourt is awarded. Chef Louis Grondard makes a prize-winning salad.

1 cup julienned beets
1 cup chopped green bean
  (1-inch pieces)
8 asparagus spears, cut into

1 tablespoon diced chives
8 cups mixed greens
Vinaigrette a la Drouant
  (recipe below)

4-inch lengths	1 melon, cut into 1-inch balls
1 julienned cucumber	4 tomatoes, cored and quartered
1 cup quartered artichoke hearts	

Place a steamer basket in a saucepan over boiling water. Add beets, green beans, and asparagus and cover. Steam for 3 minutes. Drain and set asparagus aside. Transfer beets and green beans to a medium bowl. Add cucumber, artichoke hearts, and chives, and toss gently.

Divide salad greens between four plates. Top each with beet mixture and season lightly with Vinaigrette a la Drouant (recipe below). Make a circle around each salad with four melon balls and four tomato wedges. Make a cross with four asparagus tips, with the tips at the center of the salad and the cut ends extending toward the melon balls.

VINAIGRETTE A LA DROUANT

Juice of half a lemon	salt and pepper to taste
2 tablespoons olive oil	

Whisk lemon juice and olive oil together in a small bowl. Add salt and pepper to taste.

SALAD OF ROASTED PUMPKIN, YAM, AND ROCKET

The Atlas Bistro, East Sydney, Australia

SERVES 4

$\mathcal{T}$he Atlas is a simple, airy upstairs room, that is extremely popular at lunchtime. Roasting brings out a delicious sweetness from the pumpkin and yam. Australian pumpkins are gray on the outside and orange on the inside, and used much more commonly than the American variety.

8 cups arugula (rocket)	2 cups diced pumpkin or squash
2 tablespoons pumpkin seeds	(1/2-inch chunks)
vegetable oil	salt and pepper to taste
2 cups diced yam (1/2-inch chunks)	Balsamic Vinaigrette (recipe below)

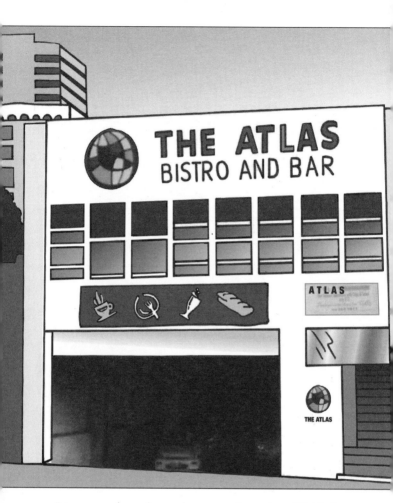

Rinse arugula under cool water and pat dry. Divide between four serving plates. Set aside.

Add pumpkin seeds to a pan and dry roast over medium heat for a few minutes until the seeds start to pop. Remove from heat and set aside.

Add oil to a roasting pan to a depth of 1/4 inch and place on stove over very high heat. Add the diced yam and sauté until brown. Transfer to a plate covered with a paper towel to drain. Next add the pumpkin and sauté until brown or even black at the edges. Drain thoroughly and add to the diced yam.

Mix the yam and pumpkin together and divide between the four arugula-covered plates. Sprinkle I 1/2 teaspoons of pumpkin seeds over each plate. Add salt and pepper to taste. Season with Balsamic Vinaigrette (recipe below) and serve.

BALSAMIC VINAIGRETTE

2 tablespoons olive oil   salt and pepper to taste
1 tablespoon balsamic vinegar

Whisk all ingredients together and serve.

THE EDGE VEGETARIAN SALAD

The Edge, East Sydney, Australia

SERVES 8

*T*he Edge is in a trendy part of East Sydney and has a high ceiling, wood floor, and pale yellow walls. What makes this salad special is the combined flavors of roasted squash, avocado, and new potatoes.

4 cups peeled and seeded butternut squash
   or pumpkin, cut into 1-inch cubes
olive oil
1 teaspoons each: dry oregano, basil,
   and marjoram
sprinkling of fresh ground pepper
3 cloves garlic, unpeeled
1 small onion, peeled and cut in quarters
3 medium potatoes, cut into 1-inch cubes
3 cups whole or chopped green beans,
   steamed 2 minutes

1 pound beets, steamed until
   tender and chopped (3 cups)
1/2 small red onion, thinly
   sliced (1/3 cup)
1/2 cup canned pitted black
   olives, sliced
1 head leafy lettuce or 4 cups
   mixed greens, coarsely
   chopped
4 avocados, peeled and cut into
   wedges dipped in lemon juice

OPTIONAL GARNISHES:

cherry tomatoes, halved   sautéed mushrooms
croutons   grilled eggplant, thinly sliced
artichoke hearts

Preheat oven to 400 degrees F.

Roasting squash: Toss the squash cubes in enough olive oil to coat. Sprinkle with oregano, basil, marjoram, and fresh ground pepper. Add garlic and 1 peeled and quartered onion. Roast for 30-40 minutes, remove the garlic and onion and let cool before adding to salad ingredients.

Roasting potatoes: Toss the potato cubes in a small amount of olive oil, salt, and fresh ground pepper. Place in a roasting pan lightly brushed with olive oil. Roast for 1 hour and let cool before adding to salad ingredients.

Toss the cooled roasted squash and potatoes, green beans, beets, red onion, and black olives. Toss the mixed greens with the Edge Salad Dressing (recipe below) and use the greens as a bed for the mixed roasted vegetables. Drizzle a touch more dressing on top, if desired, and garnish with avocado wedges.

THE EDGE SALAD DRESSING

2/3 cup extra virgin olive oil   1 tablespoon Dijon mustard
1/3 cup balsamic vinegar   salt and fresh pepper to taste

Whisk the ingredients together. The dressing will solidify if refrigerated, so be sure to leave time to bring the dressing back to room temperature before tossing with the salad.

Main Dishes

WARM WILD MUSHROOM STRUDEL
WITH BABY GREENS AND BALSAMIC OR WALNUT VINAIGRETTE

212 Market Restaurant, Chattanooga, Tennessee

SERVES 8

The 212 Market Restaurant was started by 72 year-old Marguerite Moses, along with her daughters Susan and Sally. Its balcony overlooks the sunny street and, a little further along, the stone brewery next to the river.

½ cup shiitake mushrooms
½ cup portobello or morel mushrooms
½ cup button mushrooms
2 tablespoons olive oil

2 tablespoons shallots
4 ounces filo dough
white wine, thyme, salt, and
   pepper to taste

Slice the mushrooms and sauté in olive oil with shallots. Add salt and pepper to taste. Add white wine and gradually let most of the liquid simmer away. Then chill.

Spread out a layer of filo dough. Brush a bit of oil on top (or use a spray bottle). Sprinkle with thyme and top with two more layers of filo dough, topping each with a tiny bit of oil and thyme.

Put the sautéed mushrooms on top of the filo dough and roll into a cylinder, and bake. Slice into 1 1/2-inch lengths.

The strudel can be made in advance and reheated when desired in a closed container in an oven. Serve with Balsamic or Walnut Vinaigrette (recipes below) on a bed of greens.

BALSAMIC VINAIGRETTE

1/4 red onion
1/2 sprig fresh thyme
1/4 sprig fresh basil
1/4 cup parsley
1/3 cup cilantro

1/4 cup red pepper, roasted
1/8 cup tomato paste
1 cup balsamic vinegar
2 cups peanut oil
salt and pepper to taste

Pureé the onion, thyme, basil, parsley, cilantro, and red pepper. Add tomato paste and vinegar. Then add oil in a slow, steady stream. Salt and pepper to taste.

WALNUT VINAIGRETTE

4 ounces walnut oil (or combined with
   olive oil)
4 ounces walnuts, toasted
2 ounces vinegar
salt and pepper to taste

1/2 teaspoon sugar
1 ounce water
2 tablespoons each: chives,
   parsley, tarragon

Emulsify in blender.

FAJITAS VEGETARIENS

Le Texan, Monte Carlo, Monaco

SERVES 4

*T*he owners of Le Texan brought a healthy dose of Dallas to this popular Monte Carlo restaurant.

2 zucchini, cut into quarters lengthwise,
  then into 1-inch pieces
2 carrots, cut into halves lengthwise,
  then into 1/2-inch slices
1 tablespoon olive oil
1 medium onion, coarsely chopped

2 cups brown mushrooms,
  cleaned, stems removed,
  and cut into 1/4-inch slices
salt and pepper to taste
1/4 cup Muscadet
8 tortillas

Steam the zucchini and carrots until crisp-tender (don't over-cook), and set aside. Heat olive oil and sauté onions until almost tender, then add mushrooms and sauté mixture until the mushrooms begin to brown. Mix all ingredients, add salt, pepper, and Muscadet, and grill under the broiler for a few minutes. Diners roll the mixture into a tortilla with guacomole and Pico de Gallo (recipe follows).

Pico de Gallo au Texan

FOR 8 FAJITAS

4 ripe Roma tomatoes, chopped
1 medium-large sweet onion,
 such as vidalia or red, chopped

1/4 cup chopped cilantro
1/2 large sweet red pepper,
 chopped

Mix all ingredients and let sit at least 1 hour before serving.

Jalapeno Burrito

The Mexican Village, Fargo, North Dakota

SERVES 5

The Mexican Village restaurant, in Fargo, North Dakota, has the best burrito in the world. Why would a restau-

rant closer to Canada than Mexico have such terrific cuisine? Delicate combinations make these recipes absolutely delightful.

2 1/2 cups dried pinto beans
6 cups water
2 onions, diced
1 green onion, diced

salt to taste
2 jalapeno peppers, sliced
10 flour tortillas

Wash and drain the beans. Add the water, onions, and an optional pinch of salt. Bring to a boil. Cover, and simmer (adding more water if necessary) until beans are tender and will mash readily (approximately 3 hours). Drain and mash beans with a potato masher or electric mixer. Add jalapenos.

Warm tortillas one at a time for a few seconds over a hot burner. Roll a small amount of beans in a tortilla. Cover with Red Chili Gravy (recipe below) and garnish with green onions.

RED CHILI GRAVY

2 teaspoons chili pepper*
1/4 teaspoon paprika
1/2 teaspoon salt (optional)
1 tablespoon oregano
1/2 teaspoon cayenne pepper
2 tablespoons coarsely chopped cilantro**

1/4 onion, chopped
1/2 clove garlic
1/2 cup tomato sauce
2 cups water
3 tablespoons flour
3 tablespoons vegetable oil

Combine spices, cilantro, onion, garlic, tomato sauce, and water in a saucepan. Bring to a boil. Place flour in a bowl and stir in vegetable oil. Add this to the gravy mixture, and again bring to a boil, stirring frequently as sauce thickens slightly. Serve over burrito.

*Chili pepper is not chili powder, which is a spicy combination of chili pepper, cumin, and other ingredients. It is also not the hot crushed red pepper that is sometimes found in shakers in Italian restaurants. If you have trouble finding chili pepper locally, it can be ordered from Pendery's Taste Merchants (800-533-1870) or from Penzey's, Ltd (414-679-7207).

**Cilantro is the leaf of the coriander plant and is found in the produce department.

SPICY THAI PEANUT SATA'Y

The Ovens on Monroe Street, Madison, Wisconsin

SERVES 5-8

$\mathcal{N}$o, it's not from Thailand; it's from Wisconsin. The Ovens on Monroe Street is a bakery and restaurant featuring delightful dishes, this one in the Thai tradition.

4 cups of vegetables/fruits/nuts	1 tablespoon minced garlic
1 tablespoon water	1 tablespoon olive oil

Use any combination of broccoli, carrots, cauliflower, red cabbage, green peppers, scallions, tomatoes, mushrooms, unsalted cashew halves, cilantro, raisins, or pineapple chunks, totaling 4 cups.

Sauté the vegetable/fruit/nut mixture with the water, garlic, and olive oil. Serve over rice, topped with Peanut Sauce (recipe below).

PEANUT SAUCE

SERVES 5-8

1 cup soy sauce	1 cup lemon or lime juice
1 cup peanut butter	1/2 teaspoon cayenne
2 tablespoons minced fresh garlic	1/2 tablespoon onion powder
1 tablespoon red curry paste	1/2 tablespoon basil
1/4 cup water	1/4 teaspoon paprika
1/4 cup cooking sherry	salt and pepper to taste
2-3 dashes of Tabasco	

Mix all ingredients using a whisk or blender, until creamy. Use as a savory topping.

Special thanks to Julie Smith.

VEGETARIAN WELLINGTON

Tiddy Dols, London, England

SERVES 8

$\mathcal{T}$iddy Dols began as a bakery nearly four centuries ago and still serves traditional English meals, including this

variation on the theme. Here, we have used soy cheese and soymilk instead of the cow's milk varieties.

1 10-ounce package frozen puffed pastry (contains 2 pastry blocks)	8 ounces soy cheddar cheese, shredded

Allow 2 hours for the puffed pastry to defrost to room temperature or leave overnight in the refrigerator. Dough should feel cold to the touch.

FILLING

2 medium potatoes	water
1/4 teaspoon salt	

Slice the potatoes 1/4 inch thick. Place them in a small pot, cover with water, and add the salt. Bring to a boil and then simmer until soft, about 5 minutes. Transfer to a large mixing bowl and set aside.

2 medium carrots, julienned to 2-inch pieces	1/2 teaspoon sugar
1 tablespoon olive oil	1/8 teaspoon salt
	3 tablespoons water

Place the carrots in a small pot, and add the oil, sugar, salt, and water. Bring to a boil and simmer on medium-low heat uncovered until carrots are tender and the water has evaporated, approximately 5 minutes. Transfer to the large mixing bowl.

3 medium leeks (3 cups chopped)	water
1/2 teaspoon salt	

To wash leeks, trim off root ends and most of dark green. Split leeks lengthwise and hold under running water to remove any grit. Cut leeks into 1/2-inch pieces. Place in the small pot, cover with water, and simmer for 5 minutes until tender. Transfer to the large mixing bowl.

4 large onions (5 cups thinly sliced)	1/4 teaspoon freshly ground pepper or to taste
1/4 cup olive oil	
1/2 teaspoon salt	

In a large pan, sauté the onions with the oil, salt, and pepper until soft, approximately 10 minutes. Taste and adjust seasoning as desired. The onions should be quite peppery. Transfer to the large mixing bowl.

4 cups button mushrooms
1/4 cup olive oil

1/4 cup soymilk
salt to taste

Wash the mushrooms thoroughly, and cut into 1/4-inch slices. Place the mushrooms in a small pot with the oil. Bring to a boil and simmer uncovered on medium-low heat until all the water from the mushrooms has evaporated, approximately 15 minutes. Add the soymilk and salt to taste. Transfer to the large mixing bowl and blend all the cooked vegetables together.

PUFFED PASTRY

(each box should contain 2 pastry blocks)

On a lightly floured surface, roll each defrosted pastry dough block into a 12-inch square approximately 1/4-inch thick. Cut the rolled dough into 6-inch squares. Each block of pastry dough will make 4 6-inch squares. Arrange the cut squares on a cookie sheet.

Place 1/2 cup of the vegetable filling in the center of each square and top with 1 ounce of the shredded soy cheese. Fold each corner of the pastry into the center and seal the edges together by dipping your fingers in water and moistening the edges. Chill 30 minutes before baking. Bake for 15 minutes at 425 degrees F.

STIR-FRIED SPINACH WITH BEAN CURD AND CHILI

Singapore Hut, Clayton, Victoria, Australia

SERVES 2

1 1/2 teaspoons cornstarch
1 tablespoon vegetable stock
1 tablespoon vegetable oil, divided
1 pound fresh spinach, coarsely chopped
1 tablespoon chili paste
2 cloves garlic, minced

1/4 cup vegetable stock
8 ounces firm tofu, cut into
  1-inch cubes
3 spring onions, trimmed
  and sliced
salt to taste

Mix cornstarch with 1 tablespoon vegetable stock and set aside.

Heat 2 teaspoons vegetable oil in a wok or large nonstick skillet. Add spinach and sauté 2-3 minutes until wilted. Transfer to a plate, cover, and keep warm. Drain wok and pat dry. Add 1 teaspoon vegetable oil and sauté chili paste and garlic for 30 seconds. Add 1/4 cup vegetable stock, tofu, and spring onions. Add corn-starch mixture and cook, stirring constantly for 2-3 minutes or until mixture thickens. Serve hot on top of the spinach.

THE PARK WOK

BEAN CURD IN SWEET AND SOUR PLUM SAUCE

The Park Wok, North Sydney, Australia

1 pound tofu, cut into small pieces and drained	3 tablespoons sugar
1/2 onion, sliced	3 tablespoons vinegar
3 carrots, sliced	3 tablespoons tomato sauce
1 shallot, chopped	1 tablespoon plum sauce

Fry bean curd until golden. Add sliced onion, carrots, and shallots. Mix sugar, vinegar, tomato sauce, and plum sauce with wire whisk and add to bean curd. Heat thoroughly.

Plum sauce is available at Asian and gourmet grocery stores.

PIZZA CRUST

For the pizzas on the following pages, you can use premade pizza dough or make your own.

1 envelope dry yeast (1 tablespoon)	3 cups all-purpose flour
1-1 1/4 cups lukewarm water (105-115 degrees F)	1 teaspoon salt
	2 tablespoons olive oil

In a small bowl, dissolve yeast in 1/2 cup lukewarm water. Let stand for 10 minutes, or until frothy.

Mixing by hand: In a mixing bowl, mix the flour and salt. Add the dissolved yeast to the dry ingredients with olive oil. Using a wooden spoon to mix, add just enough of the remaining 3/4 cup lukewarm water to form a dough, adding a little more water if needed. Remove dough from the bowl to a floured pastry board. Knead for 8-10 minutes or until dough is smooth and elastic. Lightly flour the board if dough begins to stick. Form the dough into a ball.

Using a food processor: Combine the flour and salt in a food processor fitted with a metal blade. With the motor running, gradually pour yeast mixture and olive oil through the feed tube and add just enough of the remaining 3/4 cup of lukewarm water until the dough forms a ball. Let the dough spin for 30-60 seconds or until smooth and elastic.

Transfer dough to a lightly oiled bowl. Cover with a damp towel or plastic wrap and let rise in a warm, draft-free place for 1 hour or until the dough is double in bulk. You can prepare the filling while the dough is rising.

When the dough has doubled in bulk, punch it down, and knead for 15 seconds. Let the dough rest under a towel for 10 minutes before proceeding with the recipe. If you are not ready to bake after punching the dough down, set the covered bowl in a cooler place, where it will keep safely for an hour or more. You can chill or even freeze the dough, but remember to leave enough time to bring it back to room temperature so the dough can start to rise again before you form a crust and bake it.

PIZZA VERONESE

Chez Bruno, Saint-Tropez, France

MAKES 8 SLICES

*P*izza, pasta, and soups have been served to a packed house just behind the old port for more than 30 years. Owner Christian Lucy still keeps an eye on every aspect of the restaurant, from the wine selection to keeping the wood-burning stove from burning down the centuries-old building.

The Pizza Veronese gets its flavor from the combination of a wood stove and by mellowing the onions by cooking them in a saucepan with a touch of oil at high heat for a few minutes, then over a low flame for a half-hour or so before being added to a pizza. A Pizza Veronese normally includes cheese, but we left it off in this recipe, and let the onions and seasonings carry the day.

3 medium tomatoes, chopped (3 cups)
1 large onion, thinly sliced (1 1/2 cups)
3/4 cup canned black olives, drained and pitted
1 tablespoon oregano
2 tablespoons olive oil
Pizza Crust (see page 41)

Break up the tomatoes and cook them in a saucepan with a small amount of oil. In a separate pan, cook the sliced onion with a small amount of oil over a high flame for a few minutes, then reduce heat to very low and simmer for a half hour or so.

Preheat the oven to 400 degrees F. Transfer the dough to a work surface that has been dusted with flour and roll out the dough into a 14-inch circle or a 9-by-14-inch rectangle with a 1/4-inch thickness. Cover the pizza with the cooked tomatoes, a sprinkle of oil, the cooked onions, olives, and a sprinkle of oregano. Bake for 20 minutes or until golden brown and when you lift an edge you can see the bottom has crisped and is patch brown.

POTATO PIZZA WITH ROSEMARY, AND CHILI AND GARLIC OIL

The Edge, East Sydney, Australia

SERVES 4

6 cloves garlic
5 dried whole chili peppers
2 tablespoons olive oil
1 medium potato, sliced paper thin

a few sprigs of fresh rosemary
salt and pepper to taste
Pizza Crust (see page 41)

Prepare a Pizza Crust as described on page 41.

Heat oven to 425 degrees F. In a blender, add garlic and chili peppers and pulse two or three times until the mixture is coarsely chopped. Pureé and slowly add olive oil until the mixture makes a paste.

Transfer pizza dough to a work surface that has been dusted with flour and roll out the dough into a 14-inch circle or a 9 x 14-inch rectangle with a 1/4-inch thickness.

Brush the pizza crust with half of the garlic mixture. Add a single layer of potato slices, overlapping slightly. Brush with the rest of the garlic mixture. Top with sprigs of fresh rosemary, and salt and black pepper to taste. Bake in an oven for 10-15 minutes or longer, if necessary, until the crust turns a deep golden brown. Slice into eight pieces. Serve hot.

PIZZA PROVENCALE A LA CAPUCCINO

Capuccino Restaurant, Calvi, Corsica

SERVES 3-4

*T*he Capuccino restaurant is in the small seaside town of Calvi on Corsica's western coast, where swallows careen over the row of restaurants outside the old walled city.

3 1/2 cups fresh tomatoes, peeled,
  cored, and chopped
2 tablespoons olive oil
1/2 teaspoon salt

pepper to taste
4 cloves garlic, chopped
8-10 black olives
Pizza Crust (see page 41)

Prepare a Pizza Crust as described on page 41.

Preheat oven to 500 degrees F. Heat olive oil in a skillet to prepare tomato sauce. Peel and break up tomatoes, and cook them with salt and pepper in oil for five minutes.

Transfer pizza dough to a work surface that has been dusted with flour and roll out the dough into a 14-inch circle or a 9 x 14-inch rectangle with a 1/4-inch thickness.

Cover the pizza crust with the sauce, and add a sprinkling of raw garlic and a few black olives. Bake for 8-15 minutes or until crust is crispy and browned.

SPAGHETTI AGLIO-OLIO-PEPERONCINO

Due Lanterne, Ventimiglia, Italy

SERVES 4

1 pound spaghetti
1/2 cup olive oil
4 cloves garlic, chopped

2 hot or mild peppers
3 pinches of fresh parsley

Boil spaghetti until al dente. Meanwhile, cook oil, garlic, and peppers in a large frying pan on medium heat, until garlic is light gold in color.

Drain spaghetti and mix well with the oil from the frying pan. Sprinkle with fresh parsley and serve immediately.

Spaghetti au Pistou

Lou Balico, Nice, France

SERVES 4

*N*ice was part of Italy until 1860, and an Italian flavor still predominates in the city's restaurants. This recipe uses pistou, perhaps the most distinctive regional flavoring. It is a sauce made from fresh basil to season spaghetti, soups, and other foods.

8 ounces spaghetti
3 bunches fresh basil leaves
2 cloves garlic

1/3 cup pine nuts
salt and pepper to taste
1/4 cup olive oil

Cook spaghetti according to package directions. To make pistou sauce, add remaining ingredients to the blender in the above order one at a time, blending each at high speed. (The traditional recipe calls for an added 50-100 grams of grated parmesan or similar cheese, which we have omitted.)

Tip: For winter, when basil is hard to come by, chop up basil, mix into olive oil, and freeze. Also, Thai basil is purple and makes a delightful change of pace.

Pasta con Asparagi

Solo Maria, Toronto, Canada

SERVES 4

*M*aria D'Orazio brought her culinary genius and Italy's warmest smile to Toronto. In this dish, she combines two favorites. We have lightened the recipe by sautéing with water or vegetable stock instead of oil.

1-2 tablespoons water or vegetable stock	1 tablespoon chopped fresh basil
1 medium onion, chopped	1/4 teaspoon ground sage
1 28-ounce can tomatoes, chopped	8 ounces spaghetti
2 pounds fresh asparagus	

Heat water or vegetable stock in a large, non-stick pan. Add onion and sauté over medium heat for 3 minutes, until translucent. Add tomatoes, asparagus, basil, and sage. Bring to a boil, cover, and simmer for 7 minutes. Remove from heat and keep warm.

Cook pasta according to package directions, omitting any fat or salt. Drain pasta and place in a serving bowl. Add the asparagus mixture and toss. Serve immediately.

Tip: Because asparagus tips cook faster than the thicker ends, you may wish to thin the asparagus with a potato peeler or chop off the ends.

Spaghetti alla Puttanesca

Linus II, Cancun, Mexico

SERVES 4

*W*here beans and salsa ought to be the order of the day, a perfect pasta is served. Leonor Parpinel catered haute cuisine in Rome and Venice and retired to Cancun with her husband Lino. Once in Mexico, she couldn't resist turning on the stove, so they started a restaurant, and now have two. The name of the dish is not for polite company, as it suggests services for hire.

2 tablespoons olive oil	1 tablespoon chopped capers
2 cloves garlic, sliced	1 pound spaghetti
8 ounces tomato pulp, peeled, cored, seeded, and sliced	1 tablespoon chopped parsley
8 ounces black olives, pitted and sliced	salt to taste

Heat oil in a skillet. Add garlic and sauté over medium heat for 1 minute. Add tomatoes, olives, and capers. Bring to a boil, cover, and simmer for 15 minutes.

Meanwhile, cook pasta according to package directions, omitting any fat or salt. Drain and transfer to a serving bowl. Add tomato mixture and toss gently. Add chopped parsley. Serve hot.

PENNE WITH FRESH SPINACH, TOMATOES, AND OLIVES

Au Bar, Palm Beach, Florida

SERVES 4

*T*he Palm Beach nightclub had a brief moment of notoriety as William Kennedy Smith's night spot as events unfolded leading to his trial. Renamed Je Me Souviens, you'll still have to wait until close to midnight for the arrival of Palm Beach's beautiful people.

1 tablespoon olive oil	1 pound fresh spinach,
1 medium onion, chopped	coarsely chopped
2 14.5-ounce cans tomatoes, diced	1 tablespoon chopped
1/2 cup kalamata olives, pitted,	fresh parsley
sliced	8 ounces penne pasta

Heat oil in a large, nonstick skillet. Add onion and sauté over medium heat for 3 minutes. Add chopped tomatoes. Bring to a boil and then reduce heat, cover, and simmer for 20 minutes. Add sliced olives, chopped spinach, and parsley. Cook an additional 5 minutes.

Meanwhile, cook pasta according to package directions, omitting any fat or salt. Drain and transfer to a serving bowl. Add spinach mixture and toss gently. Serve immediately.

BEAN AND GRAIN BURGER

Sammy T's, Fredricksburg, Virginia

MAKES 10-12 BURGERS

*O*n the streets of historic Fredricksburg, Sammy T's serves a modern cuisine. The Bean and Grain Burger is not only tastier than a typical burger, but healthier as well.

1/2 onion, finely chopped	1/4 cup tamari
1 19-ounce can garbanzo beans, ground	1/2 teaspoon garlic powder
or coarsely chopped	1/4 cup chopped fresh parsley
3 slices whole wheat bread, blended in	1 cup cooked brown rice
food processor	1 tablespoon vegetable oil
1/4 cup tahini	1/3 cup raw wheat germ

Sauté onions in vegetable oil. Then mix all ingredients and form into patties. Coat each pattie with raw wheat germ, and grill on a non-stick surface. Serve on multi-grain roll with your favorite toppings.

Vegetables and Grains

SELECTING AND PREPARING VEGETABLES
IN THE COTE D'AZUR

Le Potager
La Marine
Saint-Tropez, France

_____

The village of Saint-Tropez is nowhere near any train line, airport, or major highway, but people arrive from every corner of the world for smooth seas, sun, and civilization. Every evening sees the yachts pulling onto the port, yielding up sailors in search of a cocktail or dinner. A plate of elegantly prepared vegetables makes a perfect summer dinner. The produce vendors at Le Potager and the chef of La Marine provide these tips on choosing and preparing vegetables.

RIPENESS

Ripeness is usually judged by color and firmness. To judge the ripeness of green beans, break one open. The broken ends should be moist, not dried out. Leeks should have a deep green color, not yellow. Cucumbers and radishes should be firm, not soft. Avocados should be slightly soft, but not mushy. The stem end ripens more slowly. Artichokes should have a full appearance. As they get older, they begin to dry out and take on a withered look.

GREEN BEANS

Start with fresh, ripe green beans. Cut off both ends and any filaments attached to them. Heat salted water to boiling first, then add beans. To preserve the deep green color, do not cover the pot. Cook for 10-12 minutes, longer for large beans. Then immediately put beans into cold water or ice to stop the cooking process. Serve cold, or gently reheat. Season with onions or vinaigrette dressing. Green beans can be frozen, provided they are cooked before freezing.

ASPARAGUS

Choose asparagus about the width of your index finger. The head of the asparagus should be neither soft nor hard. Cut off the foot and slice down the sides, starting about 2 inches below the head. Heat salted water to boiling. Then add asparagus. Larger ones will need to cook for about 5 minutes, smaller ones about 3 minutes. Then put immediately into cold water or ice to stop the cooking process.

ARTICHOKES

At La Marine, artichoke hearts are cooked in a special way. First, to a saucepan of cold water, add salt, the juice of 2-3 lemons, and 1 tablespoon flour. Next, peel the artichokes. Remove the hearts and immediately put them into the cold water to prevent discoloring. Bring to a boil and cook until just tender, about 2 minutes. Serve with lemon juice or vinaigrette dressing.

To cook the whole artichoke, simply boil in salted water (or steam) for about 40 minutes. They are ready when a knife meets no resistance in the artichoke heart.

MASHED POTATOES

Young potatoes are for french fries and medium-sized red potatoes are for steaming, but, for mashed potatoes, use white potatoes, preferably older ones which are slightly soft. Wash them well and remove the skins. Put them in water and boil gently for 40-45 minutes. When they are done, they will fall apart easily. Mash with a portion of the cooking water, along with salt and white pepper.

AVOCADOS

Avocados are not cooked, so the important factor is selection. A ripe avocado is slightly soft, but not mushy. Slice and serve with vinaigrette dressing.

LA MARINE DRESSING

La Marine, Saint-Tropez, France

1 teaspoon Dijon mustard
1 tablespoon vinegar
2 tablespoons olive oil

juice of half a lemon
salt and pepper to taste

Combine all ingredients.

POTATOES PROVENCAL

The Wagnerstüble, Dobel, Germany

SERVES 4

The Wagnerstüble is in Dobel, a small village in the Black Forest of Germany. In addition to his restaurant, Chef Roy Kieferle also has a television cooking show and provides nutrition advice to professional athletes.

10 tiny new potatoes, or larger ones
    quartered
2 tablespoons extra virgin olive oil
1 medium onion, chopped
1 medium zuchini, cut into 1/2-inch
    slices
1 red pepper, cut into strips

1 clove garlic, minced
1/2 teaspoon rosemary
1/2 teaspoon marjoram
1-2 tomatoes, peeled, de-cored
    and quartered
1/4 cup finely chopped parsley
salt and pepper to taste

Parboil potatoes in boiling water for about 5 minutes, then drain. Heat olive oil in a large frying pan, add potatoes and sauté 5 minutes. Then add onions, zucchini, and red pepper and sauté an additional 8 minutes, stirring frequently, so that the vegetables cook evenly. Then mix in the minced garlic and herbs. Finally, add the tomatoes, parsley, salt, and pepper. Heat and serve.

BASMATI-VEGETABLE-FRUIT-PAN

The Wagnerstüble, Dobel, Germany

SERVES 4

1 cup basmati rice
2 cups broccoli florets
1 19-ounce can pineapple chunks,
  drained
2 unripe bananas
1 tablespoon olive oil
1 medium onion, cubed

1 medium carrot, grated
1/2 teaspoon curry powder
salt and pepper to taste
1 tablespoon chopped parsley
1 tablespoon chopped chives
1 tablespoon chopped fresh
  basil

Cook the rice in 2 cups salted water for 20 minutes, or until done. Cut the broccoli florets into small flowers. Cut the pineapple into bite-sized pieces and the banana into large slices.

Heat the olive oil in a pan, and add the onion. Shortly thereafter, add the broccoli and carrot. Lower the heat, cover the pan and let it simmer for a few minutes. Add the curry, pineapple, banana, salt, and pepper, and fry for a few more minutes. The vegetables should not be overly tender. Add the herbs shortly before serving. Serve the vegetable mixture on rice.

Thanks to Harald Ullmann.

POTATO PANCAKES (GEMÜSEPUFFER)

Restaurante Eduardos, Cascais, Portugal

SERVES 4

PANCAKES

4 large potatoes, grated
2 carrots, grated
1 medium onion, grated

1/4 cup chopped cilantro
1/2 teaspoon salt
2 tablespoons flour (optional)

Mix ingredients, press firmly into patties, and fry in oil, pressing down occasionally while cooking. Turn and fry on other side. Serve two pancakes per person, with apple sauce.

A leek can be substituted for cilantro.

APPLE SAUCE

8 apples, peeled and coarsely chopped   8 ounces white wine or water
2 cinnamon sticks

Cover the bottom of a saucepan with 1/4 inch of white wine or water. Add the apples and cinnamon sticks. Bring to a boil, then turn down heat, and simmer 10 minutes, until the apples are almost falling apart. Blend or mash with a fork. Sweeten with sugar as needed.

MILLET BASILIC

Le Commensal, Montreal, Quebec, Canada

SERVES 4-6

FOR PREPARING MILLET

2 cups water   1 1/4 cups millet
1 teaspoon oil   1/2 teaspoon salt

Bring the water and oil to a boil. Add the millet and bring to a second boil. Cover and cook for 30 minutes or until the millet is soft. There should not be any water left.

2 tablespoons olive oil   1/2 teaspoon sea salt
2 cups diced cabbage   1/2 teaspoon pepper
1/2 pound leeks, sliced into round shapes   dash of cayenne
2/3 cup sliced zucchini   1 1/2 tablespoon tamari
3 fresh basil leaves

Heat oil. Toss the cabbage, leeks, and zucchini with the basil, salt, pepper, and cayenne. Stir until slightly cooked. Combine this mixture with the cooked millet, then add tamari, mix well, and it's ready to serve!

Desserts

BLACKBERRY COBBLER

Terra Bella, Virginia Beach, Virginia

SERVES 8

*T*his is simply the most delicious dessert in the world. It comes from Regina Hawk of Terra Bella restaurant in Virginia Beach, Virginia, whose cuisine leaves diners with such an intoxication that they barely notice the hoards of young beach-goers cruising with Jeeps and boom boxes all night long. Terra means "earth" in Italian and "temple" in Japanese.

1 1/2 cup unbleached all-purpose flour	6-7 cups fresh or frozen
scant 1/4 teaspoon sea salt	blackberries
1/2 stick frozen unsalted soy margarine	1 1/2 cups sugar mixed or sifted
5 tablespoons frozen vegetable shortening	with 3 tablespoons cornstarch
4-5 tablespoons ice water	

Preheat oven to 425 degrees F.

For the crust: Combine the flour, salt, frozen margarine, and vegetable shortening in a food processor fitted with a metal blade. Process on/off pulsing until mixture is rough-textured. Add water slowly and process until dough sticks to one side of the bowl. Gather the dough into a ball and place it between two sheets of wax paper, flattening it slightly. Refrigerate for 30 minutes.

Roll the dough out on a floured surface into a large circle about 15 inches in diameter. Place the crust over the baking dish and line the bottom and sides. Allow excess crust to drape over the edges.

Filling: Mound berries in the center of the baking dish. Sprinkle with the sugar and cornstarch mixture. Bring the pastry crust over the berries. It will not quite cover all the fruit but will leave a "vent" for the bubbling cobbler.

Bake 45 minutes at 425 degrees. Serve with vanilla tofu "ice cream."

REGINA'S VEGAN CHOCOLATE CAKE

Terra Bella, Virginia Beach, Virginia

SERVES 10

3 cups flour
2 1/4 cups sugar
1 teaspoon sea salt
2 teaspoons baking soda

1 tablespoon vanilla
2 tablespoons white vinegar
1/2 cup plus 2 tablespoons
   canola oil

2/3 cup cocoa powder   2 bananas
2 cups water

Mix together the first five ingredients and sift. In a separate bowl, blend together the water, vanilla, vinegar, and oil. Mix together both bowls, stirring 1 minute with a whisk by hand.

Preheat oven to 350 degrees. Spray two 9-inch round cake pans. Pour mixture into cake pans and bake 25-30 minutes. Be careful not to overbake.

Tofu Chocolate Pudding is spread between the cake layers and is made with the recipe below. Cut one of the cooked layers in half with a serrated knife. Spread pudding lightly over this half-layer and then top it with the half-layer that had been cut off. Then add a generous layer of pudding along with two sliced bananas. Gently place the second cake layer on top and slice this layer in half with a serrated knife. Lightly add more pudding. Wrap and chill, and cut into servings with a wet knife.

TOFU CHOCOLATE PUDDING (FOR CAKE FILLING)

2 packages soft silken tofu   3 teaspoons vanilla
3/4 cup Karo syrup   1/2 cup cocoa powder
1/2 cup sugar

Place all ingredients in processor and blend at high speed until smooth.

TARTE AUX ABRICOTS

Hotel Normandy, Deauville, France

SERVES 8

*F*rench popular singer Patricia Kaas dedicated a song to Hotel Normandy. If she had tasted the Tarte aux Abricots, she would have dedicated another song to the chef. We have followed the chef's inspiration, but beg his indulgence as we have lightened the recipe considerably by replacing the eggs and butter with vegetarian ingredients.

PREPARING THE PASTRY

1 cup all-purpose flour
1 tablespoon sugar
1/4 teaspoon salt

6 tablespoons vegetable
   shortening
4-6 tablespoons ice water

Combine the flour, sugar, and salt in a food processor. Add the vegetable shortening one tablespoon at a time and process until the mixture has the texture of coarse crumbs.

With the motor running, gradually add the ice water through the feed tube of the processor, pulsing at the same time. Add just enough water until the dough forms a ball. Cover the dough with plastic wrap and refrigerate for 1 hour.

Preheat the oven to 425 degrees F. In a 9-inch tart pan with a removable bottom, press the dough into the bottom and sides until it is 1/4-inch thick. Crimp the edges decoratively. Using the tines of a fork, prick the bottom of the dough at 1/4-inch intervals.

Cut a square of lightweight foil 4 inches larger than the diameter of your shell. Lightly grease the shiny side and line the pastry, making a pouch, shiny side down. Fill the pan with a pie weight or 1 pound of dry beans and bake the pastry shell until slightly golden 12-14 minutes. Remove the foil and weights. Using the tines of a fork, prick a few more holes in the bottom of the shell and return it to the oven and bake another 2-3 minutes.

PREPARING THE FILLING

1/4 cup soy margarine
1/2 cup white sugar
1 cup ground almonds
1/2 cup white flour

1/2 cup apricot jam
1/4 cup rum
12 fresh apricots or 1 cup dried*

*If using dried apricots, pour boiling water over them and soak for a few hours to reconstitute the fruit. If using fresh apricots, halve the fruit and remove the pits.

In a food processor, blend together the margarine, sugar, almonds, flour, jam, and rum. Spread the filling evenly in the baked tart crust. Arrange the fresh or dried apricots in a decorative pattern. Bake at 375 degrees F for 45 minutes. Glaze with more apricot jam and sprinkle with sugar.

TARTE NORMANDE

Hotel Normandy, Deauville, France

SERVES 8

This tarte is made with Calvados, an apple brandy that is the signature drink of Normandy. In Norman custom, diners stop in the midst of a meal for a glass of Calvados as an aid to the digestion. As in the Tarte aux Abricots, we have aimed to retain the flavor while taking the liberty of lightening the ingredient list.

PREPARING THE PASTRY

1 cup all-purpose flour
1 tablespoon sugar
1/4 teaspoon salt

6 tablespoons vegetable
   shortening
4-6 tablespoons ice water

Combine the flour, sugar, and salt in a food processor. Add the vegetable shortening one tablespoon at a time and process until the mixture has the texture of coarse crumbs.

With the motor running, gradually add the ice water through the feed tube of the food processor, pulsing at the same time. Add just enough water until the dough forms a ball. Cover the dough with plastic wrap and refrigerate for 1 hour.

Preheat the oven to 425 degrees F. In a 9-inch tart pan with a removable bottom, press the dough into the bottom and sides until it is 1/4-inch thick. Crimp the edges decoratively. Using the tines of a fork, prick the bottom of the dough at 1/4-inch intervals.

Cut a square of lightweight foil 4 inches larger than the diameter of your shell. Lightly grease the shiny side and line the pastry, making a pouch, shiny side down. Fill the pan with a pie weight or 1 pound of dry beans and bake the pastry shell until slightly golden 15 minutes. Remove the foil and weights. Using the tines of a fork, prick a few more holes in the bottom of the shell and return it to the oven and bake another 5 minutes.

PREPARING THE FILLING

4 apples, peeled and sliced in 1/4-inch wedges*	1/3 cup softened soy margarine
3/4 cup packed brown sugar	1 teaspoon cinnamon
1/2 cup all-purpose flour	1/2 teaspoon nutmeg
1/2 cup oats	splash of Calvados

*Use a variety of apples from spy, ida red, royal gala, golden delicious, and empire. Avoid McIntosh apples, as they become mushy when cooked.

Preheat the oven to 375 degrees F. Dip apples in lemon juice to preserve their color. Mix the brown sugar, flour, oats, margarine, cinnamon, and nutmeg, which will have the consistency of a crumbly mixture. Place the apple slices on the bottom of the shell in an attractive pattern. Sprinkle the crumble mixture on top of the apples and bake for 30 minutes on the center rack.

When done, splash on some Calvados and strike a match to it.

TARTE A LA RHUBARBE WITH COULIS

Le Mille-Feuille, Nice, France

SERVES 8

*T*his dessert comes from a tiny restaurant just off the waterfront. We have modified it to take advantage of the convenience of a food processor and to reduce the fat content.

PREPARING THE PASTRY

1 cup all-purpose flour	6 tablespoons vegetable shortening
1 tablespoon sugar	
1/4 teaspoon salt	4-6 tablespoons ice water

Combine the flour, sugar, and salt in a food processor. Add the vegetable shortening one tablespoon at a time and process until the mixture has the texture of coarse crumbs.

With the motor running, gradually add the ice water through the feed tube of the food processor, pulsing at the same time. Add

just enough water until the dough forms a ball. Cover the dough with plastic wrap and refrigerate for 1 hour.

Preheat the oven to 425 degrees F. In a 9-inch tart pan with a removable bottom, press the dough into the bottom and sides until it is 1/4-inch thick. Crimp the edges decoratively. Using the tines of a fork, prick the bottom of the dough at 1/4-inch intervals.

Cut a square of lightweight foil 4 inches larger than the diameter of your shell. Lightly grease the shiny side and line the pastry, making a pouch, shiny side down. Fill the pan with a pie weight or 1 pound of dry beans and bake the pastry shell until slightly golden 15 minutes. Remove the foil and weights. Using the tines of a fork, prick a few more holes in the bottom of the shell and return it to the oven and bake another 5 minutes.

PREPARING THE FILLING

5 cups fresh rhubarb, cut in 2-inch cubes or frozen	1 tablespoon agar agar*
1/2 cup sugar	1/4 cup water
2 tablespoons maple sugar	1 ounce Cassis

*Agar agar is a sea plant that easily replaces animal gelatin. It is sold in flakes or a sponge-like bar at health food stores and Asian markets.

Place the water in a pot. Sprinkle the agar flakes into the water, bring to a boil, and stir once to incorporate the agar. Add the rhubarb, sugar, maple syrup, and Cassis to the pot, return to a boil, and then reduce heat. Simmer uncovered until the water from the rhubarb has evaporated and the filling has the consistency of jam, approximately 1 hour. Let cool to set. Spread the cooled mixture evenly on the pie crust. Top with Coulis.

COULIS

1 1/2 pound fresh fruit (strawberries, raspberries, etc.) or 1 20-ounce bag of frozen mixed fruit	1/4 cup sugar
	2 tablespoons water

Place the fruit, sugar, and water in a pot. Bring to a boil and let simmer uncovered for 30 minutes or until the mixture has the consistency of a light syrup. Let cool and then spread the topping over the rhubarb filling.

BEIGNET DE BANANE FLAMBE

Restaurant Bonsai, Paris, France

SERVES 6

water

1/2 cup all-purpose flour

1/4 cup potato starch

6 bananas

peanut or sunflower oil for frying

brandy or liqueur of choice

Pour water into a large bowl. In a pie plate, mix the flour and starch. Cut each banana in half lengthwise.

Heat the oil in a frying pan on medium-high. Before frying the bananas, be sure the frying pan is hot enough by testing with a few drops of water which should sizzle when hitting the surface of the pan. Dip the banana slices in the water, then in the flour mixture, and shake off any excess flour. Then place the bananas in the heated pan and fry approximately 3 minutes on each side, or until they turn golden brown and crisp.

To flambe: The bananas must be piping hot or the liqueur will not light. If unsure, you can heat the liqueur in a separate little pan and then pour it over the bananas. Caution: Do not pour liqueur from the bottle directly into a flaming mixture to prevent the bottle from exploding.

Breakfasts

STRAWBERRY DELIGHT

Le Commensal, Montreal, Quebec, Canada

SERVES 4

1/2 cup raw cashew nuts
3 tablespoons fruit concentrate*

2 cups strawberries, fresh
  or frozen

Soak the cashew nuts in water for 1 1/2 hours. Combine all ingredients in a food processor until the sauce is smooth. Refrigerate one hour or more before serving. This can be eaten alone or served with pancakes, granola, fruit salad, or baked goods.

*Fruit concentrate is a liquid sweetener commonly sold at health food stores. For a milder sweetener, try apple juice concentrate.

GRANOLA AU COMMENSAL

Le Commensal, Montreal, Quebec, Canada

MAKES 14 SERVINGS

5 cups uncooked oat flakes
2 tablespoons sunflower seeds
1/3 cup diced walnuts
1/3 cup sliced almonds
2/3 cup shredded coconut
1/3 cup sultanas

1/3 cup yellow raisins
1/2 cup bran
1 teaspoon sesame seeds
1/3 cup sunflower oil
1/2 cup maple syrup

Mix all the dry ingredients together in a large bowl. Combine and slightly heat the oil and syrup. Add the liquid mixture to the dry one and mix well with your hands. Spread it on a baking sheet and bake at 350 degrees F for 15-20 minutes until dried and lightly toasted. Let it cool, then store in a sealed container in a dark place. Enjoy with soymilk.

French Toast with Fruit Syrup

Rising Flour Cafe, Asheville, North Carolina

SERVES 5-7

*I*n the heart of Asheville, North Carolina, Lou Anne Rhodes cooks up genuine, down-home, Southern cuisine that is totally vegetarian and delicious.

14 slices of bread
2 cups vanilla soymilk
1/4 cup flour
1 tablespoon sugar or other sweetener

1 - 1 1/2 tablespoons nutritional
    yeast flakes*
dash of salt
1 teaspoon cinnamon

Use a softer bread, rather than a thick, heavy bread. Mix all ingredients (except bread) in a pie pan suitable for dipping. Dip the bread slices into the mixture just enough to wet the bread, not until it is soggy and starts falling apart. Pan fry in a non-stick skillet until golden. Serve hot with Fruit Syrup (recipe below) and chopped pecans.

*Nutritional yeast flakes are available at health food stores.

FRUIT SYRUP

1/2 cup apple or grape juice
3 cups chopped fruit

2 tablespoons arrowroot
2 tablespoons water

Combine the juice and fruit in a saucepan, bring to a boil, cover, and simmer for 15 minutes. Then add arrowroot dissolved in 2 tablespoons of water. Simmer until thick. Sweeten, if desired, with the sweetener of choice. To make a smooth syrup without fruit chunks, use the juice alone, without the added fruit.

PANCAKES

Rising Flour Cafe, Asheville, North Carolina

MAKES 12 4-INCH PANCAKES

1 1/4 cups flour
1 1/2 teaspoons baking powder
2 tablespoons sugar
pinch of salt

1 tablespoon canola oil
1/2 cup soymilk
3/4 cup water

In a mixing bowl, combine the flour, baking powder, sugar, and salt. Stir to mix. Pour in the oil, soymilk, and water. Mix the batter, leaving it a bit lumpy.

Heat a non-stick or lightly oiled skillet over medium heat so that a drop of water dances on its surface. Drop batter into skillet from a large spoon to form rounds. Cook until bubbles appear in the pancake and start to pop, and the underside is golden brown. Turn and brown the other side.

For waffles, use the same batter recipe, but thicken it by using only half the liquid.

FACON BACON

Rising Flour Cafe, Asheville, North Carolina

SERVES 4

1 teaspoon fennel seed
1 teaspoon cumin seed
2 1/2 teaspoons soy sauce
3 cloves garlic, crushed
dash of pepper

1 cup water
8 ounces (227-gram package)
    tempeh, sliced into bacon
    shapes

Toast fennel and cumin in a dry skillet over medium heat. Then grind the spices and return to the skillet. To the skillet, add the soy sauce, garlic, pepper, and water. Set skillet to simmer. Add the sliced tempeh and simmer 15-20 minutes. Then place the tempeh on non-stick or oiled cookie sheet, and broil until crisp (about 7-8 minutes), then turn and broil again.

The marinade will keep for one week refrigerated.

SOUTHERN SOY SAUSAGE

Rising Flour Cafe, Asheville, North Carolina

MAKES 8 SAUSAGES

2 cups cooked soybeans	1 teaspoon allspice
3/4 cup whole wheat flour	1/4 teaspoon salt, or to taste
1/4 cup wheat germ	1/4 teaspoon cayenne pepper
3 tablespoons nutritional yeast flakes	1 tablespoon turbinado sugar
1 teaspoon fennel seeds	2 1/2 tablespoons soy sauce
1 teaspoon sage	1 1/2 tablespoons Dijon mustard
2 teaspoons oregano	1/2 cup + 2 tablespoons water

Cooking soybeans: Cover the beans with water and soak overnight in the refrigerator. Drain, rinse, and place in a pot. Cover the beans with fresh cold water, and bring to a boil. Reduce heat and simmer for 3 - 3 1/2 hours until the beans are soft and tender.

Using a food processor, finely chop the soybeans. Add the remaining ingredients to the food processor and blend well. Wrap the mixture in foil in a sausage shape, about 5 inches by 2 inches. Steam foil-wrapped links in a double boiler or steamer pot for 1 1/2 hours. If you prefer, you can use a 16-ounce can as a mold, cooking in water halfway up the side of the can for 1 1/2 hours.

Remove the sausage from the form and cut it into 1/2-inch slices. Lightly grease a skillet and pan-fry the sausage slices on medium-high heat until golden crisp, approximately 7 minutes on each side.

Tips: Sausages can be split down the center and grilled until golden crisp on the outside. Serve on a bun with mustard and sauerkraut.

To make "meat balls," form the mixture into 1-inch balls before steaming. Serve with spaghetti and tomato sauce.

*Nutritional yeast flakes are available at health food stores.

BLACK BEANS WITH SALSA ON TOAST

Maya Caribe, Cancun, Mexico

SERVES 2

*I*n the 1970s Cancun was a speck on the map of Mexico's Yucatan peninsula. But long white beaches, turquoise waters, year-round sun, and quick flights to the U.S. turned it into one of the most successful fun spots anywhere.

At Maya Caribe, you can fall out of your hotel bed onto the beach, and be served the local breakfast of beans with toast. The salsa is a real eye-opener.

1 cup dry black beans
salt, garlic powder, and cumin to taste
1 teaspoon thinly sliced jalapenos

1 large tomato, diced
1/4 cup diced onions

Start with black beans. You can boil them from scratch for about 2 hours after soaking overnight. Do not undercook. After cooking, season them with salt, garlic powder, and cumin. Or you can make life easier and simply use canned beans.

Heat and mash the beans, and serve with salsa.

For the salsa, mix the jalapenos, tomatoes, and onions, adjusting amounts to taste.

Serve the beans and salsa on toast or with tortillas.